A HISTORY OF THE ARTS IN MINNESOTA
edited by WILLIAM VAN O'CONNOR

John K. Sherman

MUSIC AND THEATER IN
MINNESOTA HISTORY

THE UNIVERSITY OF MINNESOTA PRESS
Minneapolis

On May 11, 1858, Minnesota became the thirty-second state to enter the Union of the United States of America. This work is published in cooperation with the Minnesota Statehood Centennial Commission in commemoration of this historic event.

Music and Theater in Minnesota History

John K. Sherman

MUSIC AND THEATER IN MINNESOTA HISTORY

PROBABLY music has existed in what is now Minnesota for almost as long as the area has been populated, with its first expression coming from human throats in some kind of rhythmic or heightened speech. The primeval forests and hills must have echoed, at times, to the chants of the mound builders or those earlier aborigines who lived in the dim aeons of Minnesota's antiquity. But we can only speculate on what that primitive music sounded like on the basis of the relatively recent songs of the Sioux and Chippewa, which might well be the sophisticated end-product of a development starting with crude throat noises hardly definable as music at all.

Indian music, now dying out as the Indian is absorbed (in various states of segregation) by the conquering and occupying whites, is wholly outside the stream of Western music and strange and mostly meaningless to Western ears. It has been adapted to Western uses by processes of reshaping, building up, and sweetening, as in such disparate compositions as Coleridge-Taylor's cantata *Hiawatha's Wedding Feast*, Victor Herbert's opera *Natoma*, and Thurlow Lieurance's song "By the Waters of Minnetonka"; but Western it is not. We may indeed be prompted to ponder its uncanny kinship to Eastern music—not, certainly, in respect to complexity and sophistication but in the way musical sounds are

3

produced. We hear, in Indian music, the wavering tone and uncertain pitch, the throaty voice production, the repeated themes and insistent percussion that characterize much Oriental music. If more is ever known of the hypothetical migrations to America from Asia via Bering Strait, this similarity may be cited as corroborating evidence that such migration took place.

At any rate, the assertion may be hazarded that music, wherever it came from, was the first of the arts to make its stake in the Minnesota region, with the dance, accompanied by pounding rhythms, in all likelihood a close partner.

Most of what we know about Sioux and Chippewa music comes from the tireless research of the late Frances Densmore of Red Wing, who spent a lifetime recording Indian music of the United States. Her approach was coolly scientific and analytical; she had a good ear and an inquiring mind less interested in the "art," if any, of these songs than in their textual meanings and structural characteristics. Her diplomacy and tenacity enabled her to gather, as a permanent record of a dying musical language, some 3,600 Indian songs. Using primitive equipment (most of her recording was done with wax cylinders in the earlier years of this century), she persuaded often reluctant and suspicious members of Indian communities to sing into her portable horn, and reported her findings in scholarly articles and monographs that thoroughly document American Indian music of the late nineteenth and early twentieth centuries.

Music among the Indian tribes in Minnesota, as elsewhere, was largely functional, not the recreative activity it is for most of us today. It usually had a hard practical purpose, stemming from the Indian's belief that certain musical phrases linked with certain words could summon unseen forces to work beneficially for him and his tribe. A special class was the "dream song," whose secret words had magical properties and which supposedly was given to an individual by his guardian spirit while he was sleeping, or in a state of trance induced by fasting or self-hypnosis.

In most cases the songs were ensemble and ceremonial, and they were primarily a man's art, although the women in Sioux tribes often joined in the dance group. Instruments—drums, rattles, flutes, and whistles—were rarely played by themselves; usually they accompanied the songs, which with this support took on strongly marked rhythms. The "key," if it could be called that, was often minor. A few songs were solo: the medicine man and occasionally a "professional" singer seated at his drum were heard alone. But music and the dancing that went with it were essentially a group activity and could be said to be the Indian's equivalent of church, art, theater, poetry, and games; their power was that of release and uplift.

Listening to the songs, monotonous and narrow in their melodic range, one can only guess at the poetic imagery their words often contain, at their mystic view of nature and man's identification with it. Some of Miss Densmore's translations have the simplicity of Chinese poems. A dream song has these words:

> One
> wind,
> I am master of it.

Another, concerning the master of the sky who rules the storm, reads in English:

> From the half
> of the sky
> that which lives there
> is coming, and makes a noise.

More congenial and familiar to our ears are the songs that the white man brought with him to Minnesota, from the time the first French explorers penetrated the Upper Mississippi wilderness through the epoch of the voyageurs and fur traders and continuing to the mid-nineteenth-century surge of settlement. Many of these songs are now lost or forgotten, but some survive.

The first importation of Western music into Minnesota about which we know anything definite came by way of the voyageurs, those hardy French-Canadian canoemen and guides who plied the waters of Lake Superior and ventured into the streams and rivers of this then "far west" area. The voyageur flourished for more than a century, disappearing at about the time the settler from the east and Europe began to move west in the 1850s to find a new home. Of this dauntless and resourceful adventurer, Grace Lee Nute has written: "he appeared speeding over lakes, advancing cautiously up narrow creeks, toiling over portages, cracking his whip over the heads of his dogs, laughing down rapids, fiddling in log forts, and singing wherever he was."

Such a man, often alone, living by his wits and skill in the uncharted wilds, must have found music not only a boon but an occupational necessity. His songs of love and sunny climes, of home and of adventure, some bawdy and some sentimental, carried imagery of the graces and pleasures of the ordered world he had left behind, and usually were a work aid as well. The rhythm of the voyageurs' songs was often set by the stroke of the paddle, thus (as in many Negro work songs of the south) making a drudging, repeated physical operation less arduous. When together, voyageurs sang in unison in their boats, the steersman often starting with the verse and the rest joining in the refrain. Good singers among voyageurs were accounted valuable employees by the fur-trading companies that hired them, their skill in this morale-building accomplishment earning them a premium in pay.

One of the best known and most popular of the voyageurs' songs — and still a French-Canadian favorite — was "A la claire fontaine," a haunting ballad whose tenderness and nostalgia differed markedly from the rough conditions of the voyageurs' existence.

In contrast to the voyageurs' sing-while-you-work songs, whose lineage can be traced to the motherland France and even to medieval balladry, were the loggers' songs and shanty-boy ballads of Minnesota's north woods, of mostly Anglo-Irish ancestry. These yarns-to-music were an after-dark diversion following the long day's work. The husky and hardy lumberjacks gathered in their bunkhouses and sang of the bold worker and his adventures and the dangers of his job. The songs followed oft-used narrative patterns; one of the most popular, "The Jam on Gerry's Rocks," started with this typical summons:

> Come all you jolly fellows, wherever you may be,
> I hope you'll pay attention and listen unto me.

Meanwhile, and earlier, on the prairies and rolling country farther south, another stream of "homemade" balladry from still another source had flowed into the state with the influx of immigrants from all parts of Europe, particularly from Scandinavia and Germany. Westering home seekers from these lands sang their own kind of song, topical ballads that told sad or heroic stories and recalled the pangs of leaving Old Country scenes. To simple tunes were chronicled the adventures and setbacks of moving to a new land, the hopes of a fine and free life awaiting the settler: homespun laments and sagas and jingles, buoyant and dolorous.

Theodore C. Blegen has written of the singing immigrant and the songs of the Norwegians who flocked to America by the hundreds of thousands from 1825 on. Noting the Norwegians' native love of music, he has commented that "they cannot—or at least they could not—embark upon a popular movement without singing about it in one way or another, either in praise or in condemnation."

All this, if not folk music, was music of the folk of Minnesota's pre-concert days, before music was organized and institutionalized as an art, an educational subject, a public performance medium, and a cultural commodity that could be bought and enjoyed by the nonparticipant.

The middle of the nineteenth century marks roughly the beginning of this change, when scattered settlements began to grow into villages and the marks of civilization began to appear in dim and crude form. The settlers brought music with them, not only the topical songs of immigration and the period's popular ballads but the voices, and instruments, through which music of an increasingly higher artistic level could be produced.

Melodeons, pianos, and harpsichords were trundled overland in wagon trains and shipped upriver to the port of St. Paul. Guitars, more portable, were advertised and sold locally. The violin, cornet, and flute began to be heard in domestic parlors and public meeting places, and in churches the superior voices in singing congregations were soon mobilized into quartets for part-singing of hymns. One of the earliest and best known of these ensembles was the Congregational Church Quartet of Minneapolis, on call during the fifties and sixties for all kinds of occasions, secular and religious, to which a foursome of well-blended voices added distinction.

Easiest to organize and filling both a social and a musical need were the singing societies, mostly of Germans and Scandinavians but representing many other European strains as well, which preserved at that time and for many years their racial identity and tongue. The singing pioneer became the singing member of groups, and soon the choral director and vocal teacher came on the scene. In fact the music teacher—usually a humble and semiprofessional or part-time practitioner of his art—and the pioneer pastor who insisted on making music a part of church worship and service were key figures in Minnesota's early musical manifestations, and in the steady improvement of its musical product.

It was in the future Twin Cities (not "twin" then but the prairie-separated communities of St. Paul and St. Anthony) that concert music made its start, and the standards of the older east and the influence of European tradition were not long in making themselves felt in these music-hungry young settlements.

St. Paul being the older of the two, the terminus of upriver travel, it made earlier progress, and even in the 1850s it had three or four small halls where music was frequently performed. In 1858 four string players—Gustav Hancke, Herman Mocklett, Conrad Zenzius, and George Seibert—organized an informal quartet with which to entertain themselves and their friends, and from this group five years later sprang the St. Paul Musical Society, a small orchestra which was to survive for a quarter century as one of the leading instrumental ensembles of the state. It is likely that its performance of a Haydn symphony in 1863 provided the first hearing for Haydn or for any other eighteenth-century composer in Minnesota.

The society's fame spread and it was invited to give concerts across the river and in other nearby towns. In 1871 it brought to Minneapolis, which had just taken the older St. Anthony into the municipal fold, the first local performance of two movements of

Beethoven's Second Symphony, part of a program that dedicated the newly built Academy of Music on Hennepin Avenue. Thus Minneapolis' first and for some time its best orchestral playing was supplied by its sister city. The favor was to be returned forty-three years later when the Minneapolis Symphony Orchestra started a series of concerts in an orchestra-less St. Paul.

Like St. Paul, Minneapolis from its earliest years had resolutely made its own music. In the early fifties B. E. Messer, sign painter and violinist who had started his career teaching children of 8 to 15 to sing, free of charge, produced a costumed fantasy, *Flora's Festival*, in St. Anthony's Congregational church. Later he helped form the town's first instrumental group, the Quintette Club, comprising players of violin, piano, cello, cornet, and flute — a true (if small) orchestral forerunner. The pianist of the club, C. A. Widstrand, was to engage in a long career as teacher, organist, and leading music merchant of Minneapolis.

In the sixties the Germans formed the Harmonia Society, a long-lived and respected singing organization, and in 1868 the Musical Union, a choral group with a small instrumental complement, staged a lavish production of George Root's oratorio *Belshazzar's Feast, or The Fall of Babylon*, which drew eager attendance from a large surrounding area. Costumed choral works of Oriental tinge like this and Bradbury's nationally popular *Queen Esther* continued to be the rage through the sixties and into the seventies.

Minneapolis, not to be outdone by its rival across the river, set up a shaky equivalent of St. Paul's Musical Society in 1872, but it did not last long. The Minneapolis Musical Society at its grand opening played to a small audience under the dynamic Ludwig Harmsen, a German-born musician who was to become much in demand as an organist, choral director, and teacher. The society lasted for only two or three concerts. Its successor was the firmer-based Orchestral Union, which in time boasted twenty-two instruments (including what the local press called a "tuber") and which persisted almost through the rest of the decade.

St. Paul's George Seibert, meanwhile, had taken over the St.

George Seibert

Frank Danz, Jr.

Early orchestral music makers of the Twin Cities

The summer band of Frank Danz, Jr.

Paul Musical Society as director and had also organized the Great Western Band and Orchestra. By arrangement with his brother-in-law, a Fort Snelling band leader named Frank Danz, a Minneapolis version of the Great Western, with Danz in charge, was established. This marked the start of a long and significant chapter in Minneapolis' musical life.

With the name of Danz is associated Minneapolis' hard-won and eventually deep-rooted status as an "orchestra city," where symphonic music established a home and claimed the sustained interest of the concertgoing public. For it was Danz and particularly his determined son, Frank Danz, Jr., an accomplished violinist, who taught the young city to listen, sometimes grudgingly, to orchestral music—this in a period when opera and operetta troupes were invading the state in ever increasing numbers.

The Danz concerts, under the senior Danz, had their start in 1880 in the Academy of Music under the Great Western label but soon shifted to the new Turner Hall on the near north side, where the organization became identified as Prof. Danz's Orchestra. Four years later father Danz wooed his son away from Theodore Thomas and the New York Philharmonic and proudly saw him take the helm of the then sixteen-piece orchestra.

Turner Hall's beer garden atmosphere and predominantly German clientele were deserted by Danz in 1886 for the more centrally located Harmonia Hall, in the lower loop. Here, a bid was made for a larger segment of the musically cultivated population, and here into the nineties the Danz concerts served and intensified the city's appetite for concert music.

Frank Danz, Jr., an imperturbable, moon-faced man with down-sweeping mustache, was a prototype of the conductors who were to link Minneapolis' name with superior orchestral achievement in the twentieth century. As did his more famous successors, he often had to deal with apathy and wavering support, but his tenacity of purpose and his standards of programming and orchestral technique educated a town for what it finally had to have—good orchestral music, regularly purveyed.

Of course the Danz orchestra in Minneapolis and Seibert's concerts in St. Paul were only part of the musical upbringing that the Twin Cities and the rest of the state submitted to as taste improved and interests were widened by all manner of musical visitations from the east and overseas.

The primitive days of bell ringers and singing families, of zither players and cornet bands and gaudy-garbed cantatas, were succeeded in the century's last two decades by more sophisticated and sumptuous entertainment. Thirty different opera companies, returning again and again, swooped on Minnesota during the eighties alone; these ranged from small troupes in opera potpourris to ensembles featuring the famed throats and chests of the day.

This was the heyday of such operatic *grande dames* as Nilsson, Patti, Nordica, Calvé, Eames, Lehmann, and Sembrich, most of whom traveled conscientiously and conspicuously to the far reaches of their orbits. Minnesotans were possessively proud of Swedish-born Olive Fremstad, the mezzo-soprano who spent her girlhood in Minneapolis and became one of the queens of grand opera. Outstanding instrumentalists were in copious supply: violinists Wieniawski (who had first come in 1873), Reményi, Sarasate, and the diminutive Camilla Urso; pianists Teresa Carreño and D'Albert, keyboard stars of the nineties, and finally the young prodigies Ignace Paderewski and Josef Hofmann. All of them included Minnesota on their circuits.

The glories of fine orchestral playing that the Danz and Seibert concerts aimed at were eloquently realized in the frequent visits of Theodore Thomas and his orchestra and such engagements as the epical appearance in 1890 of the Boston Symphony Orchestra, conducted by Arthur Nikisch. They played in Minneapolis' echoing Coliseum which had just been equipped with arc lights, a new invention that hissed.

Two years later Minneapolis heard its first all-Wagner program as played by Danz, who was audacious when he wanted to be and who anticipated by a year a similar program presented by the noted Anton Seidl and his Metropolitan Opera Orchestra in 1893. But Wagner's hypnotic harmonies had long since penetrated the upper midwest: eighteen years before, the Mendelssohn Quintette had sung the bridal chorus from *Lohengrin*, providing what was then termed a glimpse into "the music of the future."

The role of the musical club, a peculiarly American institution organized by energetic women who viewed civic uplift in terms of musical improvement, is an important facet of our story. Perhaps the most significant incident in nineteenth-century St. Paul was the founding of the Schubert Club, which in 1958 claimed the distinction of being the oldest musical club in the state. During the 1870s a number of music-minded St. Paulites held meetings and concerts in homes and finally, in 1882, decided to formalize their activities by giving their group a name, the Ladies' Musicale. In 1891 the name was changed to the Schubert Club, and during the ensuing decade choral and orchestral units were formed, duties and activities were much expanded, and such noted artists as Xaver Scharwenka and Eugène Ysaye lent luster to the club's calendar of events.

Similar if smaller-scaled activity across the river was exemplified by the Lorelei Club, also an all-female effort, which amounted to little until 1892 when forty of its members, aroused to action by Laura Carroll Dennis, decided on bigger and better aims and reorganized themselves as the Ladies' Thursday Musicale. The name was later changed to the Thursday Musical, and the organization soon vied with St. Paul's Schubert Club in bringing noted artists, including the ever popular Theodore Thomas, to the Twin Cities.

The third outstanding club in the state to promote good music as a community project—one also still in existence and thriving— was the Matinee Musicale of Duluth, founded in 1900. The pattern was repeated here of sponsoring concert series by noted persons and groups; performances by Alma Gluck, Harold Bauer, the Kneisel Quartet, and Walter Damrosch's New York Symphony were among its early events. At the same time, as was the case with the Twin Cities clubs, local interest was built up by implementing the sound theory that music in performance and knowledgeable listening react on each other to mutual stimulus and improvement.

Before lifting the curtain on the twentieth century, we must pause once more in the busy 1890s in Minneapolis. This was an im-

Emil Oberhoffer

Elbert L. Carpenter

Olive Fremstad

portant seeding time, for two new organizations destined to change the shape of Minnesota music took root in that decade. One of them was the Apollo Club, a male choral organization which had engaged as its director a promising and impecunious Bavarian musician named Emil Oberhoffer. The other was the Philharmonic Club, a mixed choral group which had sprung out of a half-silly, half-serious organization calling itself the Filharmonix.

The Filharmonix at the start plucked banjos and mandolins and formed a glee club but soon, impressed by public attention, looked to loftier goals. In 1896, its glee club was singing well enough to justify the change of name to the more dignified Philharmonic Club, and four years later it lured Oberhoffer away from the rival Apollo Club. Its purpose was to stage more ambitious and substantial choral works under his direction, which it proceeded to do. Under Oberhoffer the club's artistic stature grew; in the next three years performances were given of such works as Handel's *Messiah*, Haydn's *Creation*, Verdi's *Requiem*, and Saint-Saëns' *Samson and Delilah*. The latter was precedent-shattering in its use of a complement of instrumentalists from Thomas' Chicago orchestra.

Oberhoffer during this period was increasingly distressed by the unreliability of his makeshift orchestral forces, whose members were hired on a temporary basis; the professionals were often absent from the public performance after appearing at rehearsals, the amateurs (who played for the fun of it) just as often missing when most needed. Accompanying this discontent with a haphazard organization was Oberhoffer's growing ambition to set up a permanent orchestra that not only would be on call for choral performances of the Philharmonic but by providing all-orchestral fare would raise its status from choral accompanist to symphony orchestra.

The Philharmonic's 1902–3 season was so successful that the issue of a permanent and efficient orchestra came to a head in the spring of 1903, and the organization of the Minneapolis Symphony was forthwith achieved and announced, its first season to start the succeeding fall.

The first concert of the new organization was played on November 5 with dependable Frank Danz and his men strategically placed in a group of about fifty musicians assembled on the stage of the Exposition Building, which had been hastily disguised as a concert hall. An expensive soprano (Marcella Sembrich, who received $1,800) was the star of the evening, and the concert was accounted a brave beginning.

Since that chilly November evening, when the brass sounded too loud and the Moszkowski *Serenata* was played twice because the audience demanded it, the Minneapolis Symphony has survived a multitude of vicissitudes—financial, artistic, temperamental — and has grown steadily in stature.

It soon became a touring troupe which in the decades to come was to cover more ground and play in more cities and towns, more states and countries, than any other organization of its kind in the United States. In Minneapolis, after its debut, it wandered from hall to hall until the autumn of 1905 when it found a permanent home in the new Auditorium on Eleventh Street; it was to move once more in 1930, to become the first major civic orchestra associated with a university, giving regular concerts in Northrop Auditorium on the University of Minnesota campus.

Popular concerts on Sundays were launched in 1906 and young people's programs in 1911—both institutions becoming a permanent phase of the orchestra's service to the community. The "pops" over the years have had varying fortunes and now are identified as a series of nine Sunday "twilight concerts" per season, and well patronized. The young people's concerts have grown mightily, playing in 1957–58 to school children totaling 29,500 in Minneapolis and 13,500 in St. Paul.

The Minneapolis Symphony has had five regular conductors in its fifty-five years. Oberhoffer (1903–21) was the self-made conductor, the energetic dreamer, the poet-interpreter, who mixed his menus artfully out of the old and new. His Belgian successor, Henri Verbrugghen (1923–30), brought a more scholarly approach and more emphasis (sometimes dryly so) on technique. The arrival of Eugene Ormandy (1931–35) after Verbrugghen's ill health had caused an interpretive decline introduced a compelling style from

Dimitri Mitropoulos

Eugene Ormandy

Antal Dorati conducting
the Minneapolis Symphony
in rehearsal

a young maestro on the rise. The Greek Dimitri Mitropoulos (1937–48), a sometimes severe but always exciting apostle of music, gave concertgoers among other things a heady course in contemporary music. Antal Dorati (1949–   ), a Hungarian like Ormandy, has proved an able and interesting program builder and an expert in improving the orchestra's tone, texture, and technical polish. His associate, Gerard Samuel, has fulfilled many assignments, including popular and young people's concerts, with fine authority and finish in his conducting style.

The orchestra is certainly Minnesota's outstanding contribution to the world of music, its performances and recordings gaining international repute, its quality now an expected attribute. Its rise and stability are all the more noteworthy in that a city which ranked eighteenth in population in 1903 became one of only seven in the country then possessing orchestras of their own. For years it was an expensive luxury that the community could barely afford, and perhaps would not have paid for if the pocketbook and influence of E. L. Carpenter, the chief patron, had not frequently come to the rescue. For a half century its necessary deficits have been a burden that has caused periodic worry yet reared a challenge that civic spirit and determined campaigning have met.

In many ways the Minneapolis Symphony has become a model of high attainment in musical performance which has inspired emulation and set up a standard for other musical ensembles to aim at. Itself a culmination of long concern with orchestral performance and its enjoyment, growing out of the early conducting efforts of Harmsen, Danz, Seibert, and such shorter-lived Twin Cities groups as Sidwell's and Ringwald's orchestras, it has generated livelier interest and more conscientious participation in music along a wide front. School and college orchestras in the state, for example, exist in greater number and are more aware of their shortcomings than would have been the case had there been no Minneapolis Symphony concerts to hear and to imitate. Numerous civic orchestras have pridefully assumed their role of spreading the kind of fare the Minneapolis Symphony has offered and providing a constructive outlet for amateur and semiprofessional talent.

Between 1906 and 1914, there was a fully professional St. Paul Symphony Orchestra, conducted by a Mahler pupil, Walter Rothwell, and the musical rivalry of the two cities for a time took on the rather childish refrain of we've-got-a-better-orchestra-than-yours. But after eight seasons and a siege of bad management, the St. Paul orchestra had become such a financial headache to those who paid for it, and a matter of such indifference to the populace, that its affairs were liquidated. Thereafter, for fifteen years, the Minneapolis Symphony regularly played in the sister city programs that duplicated Minneapolis' Friday nights.

Over varying periods, both cities have supported, or at least listened to, other orchestras. During the depressed 1930s several instrumental ensembles rose and fell, the Minnesota Symphony, the Twin Cities Civic, and the Federal (WPA) Symphony orchestras. Later a chamber orchestra, the Northwest Sinfonietta, introduced a fresh repertoire to the Twin Cities and surrounding region, under the baton of Henry Denecke. In 1958, two civic orchestras using in varied proportion professional and advanced amateur talent were in existence—the Civic Orchestra of Minneapolis under Thomas Nee, a rising young conductor, and the St. Paul Civic Orchestra, which has functioned under several directors.

Around the state there has been both sporadic and sustained orchestral endeavor. Some orchestras have not survived but during their periods of activity gave devoted service and attracted loyal listeners. One of the longest-lived was the Hibbing-based Range Symphony Orchestra, made up of forty to sixty volunteer players, founded in 1921 by an enterprising Venetian, Luigi Lombardi, and active for nearly twenty years. The group toured northern Minnesota towns and made frequent visits to the Twin Cities. St. Cloud's civic orchestra under Erwin Hertz was supported by city taxation and held concerts for four years from 1944 to 1948. In 1957 Austin and Mankato joined the ranks of Minnesota communities starting home-grown orchestras. Rochester's record is a longer one. Its symphony orchestra in an early version started in the 1920s, for a time played under Orvis Ross, Rochester teacher and composer, and is now conducted by Harold Cooke. Made up of seventy-five musicians from all walks of life, including numerous physicians from the Mayo medical center, it offers four or five concerts a season, rehearses weekly, imports noted soloists, and (with the Rochester Oratorio Society) engages in such undertakings as Mendelssohn's *Elijah*, the Brahms *Requiem*, and annual performances of Handel's *Messiah*. The group has become southeastern Minnesota's proudest musical organization and draws both players and listeners from a wide area.

Of civic orchestras outside the Twin Cities, however, the Duluth Symphony probably occupies the premier position. Its history goes back to 1932, when a group of thirty-five jobless theater musicians and diverse part-time and amateur players decided to get together and perform music by the classical masters.

Major credit for both the idea of a permanent Duluth orchestra and its materialization must go to Alphin Flaaten, a cellist who was inspired to send a summons to all musicians of all degrees of professionalism in the area to meet for a warm-up rehearsal in an old stable back of his home. A raging blizzard delayed but did not prevent a sizable gathering made up, among others, of an Eveleth miner, a Superior clothier, a Cloquet paper mill worker (who brought his tuba), and assorted housewives, clerks, dentists, and elevator operators.

Paul Lemay, viola principal and assistant conductor of the Minneapolis Symphony, became in 1933 the Duluth group's first regular conductor, following a first season when the musicians ran their own orchestra. At the beginning of his regime he commuted the 175 miles between Minneapolis and Duluth two or three times a week. At first he worked for his expenses only, and he devoted his energies not only to preparing performances but to "selling" the orchestra to the people of Duluth through talks to service clubs and church and community groups.

Lemay conducted the Duluth Symphony until 1942, when he enlisted in the United States Air Corps. He later was killed in action over Holland. Subsequent conductors have been Tauno Hannikainen from Finland, noted Sibelius exponent; Joseph Wagner, composer-conductor who held the helm for two and a half

Hermann Herz   F. Melius Christiansen

years and staged a notable program of works by Minnesota composers; and Hermann Herz, who came from Munich via Johannesburg, South Africa, and has done much to diversify programs and strengthen the orchestra's technique. Heading an ensemble numbering eighty-five members, Herz in his seven-concert seasons has taken on ambitious choral-orchestral works and has found favor with his concertized treatments of operas. His Junior Symphony, composed of high school instrumentalists, has done much to spur music interest among the younger generation.

Orchestral performance tells far from the whole story of musical enterprise in Minnesota. Many indeed would claim that Minnesota is pre-eminently the state of choral singing. Certainly its history is longer than that of any other kind of music-making in Minnesota, going back to the singing societies and the *Saengerfests* of an early day, when singing delegates from all over the region invaded the cities for massive choral fetes. The popularity of oratorios brought vocalists and instrumentalists together at frequent intervals, and for challenging assignments. As early as 1872 Haydn's *Creation* was presented as a special feature of the State Musical Association convention.

The already mentioned Apollo Club and Philharmonic Club, formed in Minneapolis in the 1890s, illustrate characteristic civic enterprise in the formation of choral groups. But at a Norwegian Lutheran college in a small town—St. Olaf in Northfield—the state's most significant development in choral art was to take place in the early years of the twentieth century. The man who was to revolutionize choral singing, rescuing it from glee club superficiality on the one hand and dreary Lutheran hymnology on the other, was F. Melius Christiansen, a thirty-two-year-old Norwegian violinist and teacher who arrived on the St. Olaf campus in 1903, at a beginning stipend of $600 per annum.

The now-famous St. Olaf choir did not immediately spring full-fledged from his brow. Put in charge of the college's almost non-existent music department, Christiansen was given a free hand in doing whatever he thought should be done to unify music instruction and raise its standard. Emigrating as a boy from Norway, he had been in America fifteen years in 1903, except for two years spent in study at the Leipzig conservatory. He had attended Augsburg Seminary in Minneapolis in the early 1890s, and after his European sojourn returned to Minneapolis in 1899 to teach, play the organ, and conduct church choirs.

In Northfield he started by taking charge of the college band ("his first love," he was later to say), traveling with it to Norway in 1906. After further study of chorales and Lutheran hymns, many of which he reharmonized in contrapuntal style to give them more musical substance, he took over the St. John's Lutheran Church Choir, most of whose members were St. Olaf students and faculty members.

His twin interests in composition and refurbishing chorales, and his developing conducting skill (by this time he had virtually laid aside his violin) led inevitably, it may be seen now, to his pre-eminence as a choral music reformer and leader. In the spring of 1911, he was invited by an Eau Claire pastor to bring his St. John's group to Wisconsin. The invitation was accepted, other engagements in the area were quickly secured, and the choir made its first tour. For this maiden trip the group was re-christened the St. Olaf Lutheran Choir, so named as a means of clearly identifying the geographical source and academic allegiance of its members. Later, frequent trips to the east and to Europe spread the choir's name and fame.

Singing without accompaniment and early in its career achieving what critic Herman Devries termed "pitch-perfect, tone-perfect and text-perfect skill" in the most difficult classic choral music, the choir swiftly gained a reputation as something unique of its kind.

Its singing, in fact, was perfection, but a perfection gained as a result of the most gruelling work by the choristers and an almost ruthless selectivity and discipline by Christiansen. Sixty students, men and girls, were chosen in a series of tryouts (about twenty new voices grafted on to the ensemble each year as the graduates fell out), and trueness of ear was deemed as important as quality of voice. Weeding out deteriorating voices in rehearsal was as necessary as keeping out inadequate ones beforehand. Ten hours a week practice, high scholarship in other school work, non-tremolo voices capable of blending with one another (the voice, said Christiansen, should be "straight as an Indian woman's hair or a telegraph wire"), and complete memorization—these were some of the basic requirements.

Singing in the choir was a form of slavery which at the same time became a badge of high honor at St. Olaf, and has remained so since. For more than forty years the stocky, peremptory Christiansen led the group, during which he himself composed many works in the general style of German Reformation music but with his own vigorous mark upon them. On his retirement his son Olaf C. Christiansen took over the baton and has carried on, with his own conscientious and cultivated musicianship, the high ideals and technical skill his father instilled.

The St. Olaf influence — the clear and cool purity of its style and what James Huneker called "the precision of a small orchestra"— has had an overwhelming influence in the region and in the country at large. Its high standards have been adopted by many choirs and choruses of the state, even those that have wandered into secular realms and varied in their own ways the St. Olaf formula.

Another gifted son of Dr. Christiansen, Paul J. Christiansen, proved anew that exceptional *a cappella* singing could be nurtured in a small town college and brought to a high level of technical and interpretive excellence. Head of the music department of Concordia College at Moorhead, he has been director of the Concordia Choir since 1937 and, like his father before him and his brother Olaf in Northfield, has led it afield on extensive tours, including two to Europe (in 1949 and 1958), each time bringing back verbal laurels from critics and audiences. In Concordia's programs, as with other groups spiritually descended from the St. Olaf Choir, we find music that ventures from the earlier strict pattern into semi-secular and modern works.

In Minneapolis, another superior ensemble, the Augsburg College Choir, was formed in 1933 by a merging of the school's glee club and choral society and put under the direction of Henry P. Opseth, music department chairman, who served in that capacity until his death. Since 1950 the group has been led by conductor-composer Leland B. Sateren. As with many other choirs in small colleges, the pre-history of this polished group goes back to the earlier decades of the century when *a cappella* singing was developed as much by necessity as by choice: the human voice is a built-in musical instrument everyone owns without initial cost, and students' budgets are often lean. Augsburg's choir through the Opseth regime and under the tasteful and vigorous leadership of Sateren has developed smooth, unobtrusive technique, a full, warm tone, and expressive interpretation. Here again the repertoire cuts a wide swath from seventeenth century to modern.

Scarcely a college in the state, or high school for that matter, lacks a singing group of some kind, and anyone who has had fairly frequent opportunity to hear samples of their work over a long period can testify to the steady technical improvement of such groups and the increasingly high aims that actuate them.

Choral singing at St. Paul's Hamline University (under Robert Holliday) and Macalester College (under Ian Morton) must be noted for particular excellence. The Gustavus Adolphus Choir of St. Peter, led by Philip F. Knautz, thrives artistically. Such smaller Minneapolis groups as Edith Norberg's Carillon Singers, Frederic Hilary's Madrigal Singers, and James Aliferis' University Chamber Singers have shown the finesse, the sharp-focused expression, which are attainable in vocal "chamber music" when a few fine voices are carefully chosen and scrupulously drilled.

Professor Aliferis has also devoted much of his energy to the University of Minnesota Chorus, one of the largest singing bodies in the state, 250 to 300 mixed voices, which since 1946 under Aliferis (and before that under Earle Killeen) has joined the Minneapolis Symphony in such large-scale works as the Beethoven Ninth Symphony and *Missa Solemnis*, the Berlioz *Romeo and Juliet*, and the Bach *St. Matthew Passion*. One of the unusual choral phenomena on the Minnesota campus was the University Bach Society, a "town-and-gown" chorus which gave spring Bach festivals from 1934 to 1950, led by Donald Ferguson, composer, teacher, and Minnesota's most distinguished music historian. On his retirement in 1950 from the University of Minnesota music department, Ferguson moved across the river to take charge of Macalester's department of music.

The Apollo Club, mentioned earlier, has had a long and prosperous career as a civic male chorus. By arduous preparation it has risen from glee club status to achieve more than competence in assignments in difficult repertoire: Palestrina, contrapuntal Bach, and choruses from Moussorgsky's *Boris Godounov*, for example. While it retains some rollicking favorites in its current repertoire, the programs in recent years have shown a keen artistic conscience. After several shifts in leadership during its youth, the club sang long terms under Hal Woodruff and William MacPhail (a violinist who played at the Minneapolis Symphony's first concert and subsequently founded a music school) and into the 1950s was led by Ralph Williams and then James Allen, its former accompanist. It has accrued national fame through the sound track it made for one of the wide-screen Cinerama productions.

The Apollo Club's opposite number in St. Paul for several years was the Orpheus Club, conducted by Malcolm McMillan. Founded in 1919, it is now extinct.

One of the state's ablest choral conductors is Rupert Sircom, organist and choirmaster at Westminster Presbyterian Church in Minneapolis, who in the 1930s was in charge of the Twin City Symphony Chorus, a temporary adjunct of the Minneapolis Symphony that sang under Eugene Ormandy in Mahler's *Resurrection* symphony, Verdi's *Requiem*, and several other choral-orchestral offerings. Since that time Sircom has for the most part confined his choral undertakings to his church, where he has presented major works by Bach and Brahms' *German Requiem*. The Cathedral of St. Mark and Central Lutheran Church have frequently been the scenes of important musical presentations. A score or more of other churches, in the Twin Cities and through the state, could be cited for the superiority of their music groups, led by devoted professionals.

An all-female chorus founded by Mrs. H. A. Patterson, the Cecilian Singers, was for many years a bright spot on Minneapolis' musical calendar, while the Symphonic Chorus of the Twin Cities, springing up during World War II at an ammunition plant, has had an active career under Clarence Russell, a Mary Garden pupil and protégé, and later conductors, including its present leader, Bruce G. Lunkley.

Racial singing groups, so vigorous a component of the musical community in the days of the first settlers, do not attract as large a proportion of the music-minded public as they once did, but they are carrying on sturdily along modern and "Americanized" lines. By singing more songs in English translation, yet keeping alive the homeland tongues in a portion of every program, they serve as a link with Old Country culture for an English-speaking generation otherwise cut off from it. Among the older groups active today are the Norwegian Glee Club, for many years led by Carl G. O. Hansen and now conducted by Frederick Wick; the Nordkap Male Chorus under Kenneth Lower; the American Swedish Institute Male Chorus of Minneapolis, under Harold Brundin; and the Swedish Male Chorus of St. Paul, under Edwin G. Amundson.

It goes without saying that Minnesota, musically, has not been self-sufficient. The state's vitality in the art has been nourished as much from the outside as from its own initiative in musical production. From the importation of world-noted artists and organizations has been gained the experience of observing high endeavor, virtuosity, and polish in performance. The circuit today certainly is not the crowded and feverishly traveled itinerary it was in the period from the 1880s through the second decade of the twentieth century, but music has suffered far less than theater in this respect. From territorial times when Ole Bull and Adelina Patti, then a girl of thirteen, gave joint recitals in 1856, the state, despite its location off the main line of east-west travel, has been host—an eager paying host—to the gypsy brood of musicians making their unceasing rounds of the world's concert stages.

Many of the nineteenth-century visitors have already been mentioned. As we move into the twentieth century, we find the Minneapolis Symphony a major importer of talent, in its first two decades calling often upon opera singers, whose appeal to the public usually outweighed the more intellectual attraction of pianists and violinists. This practice of giving concerts allure with a prima donna soloist has gradually diminished as symphony orchestras everywhere have strengthened their proper role as exponents of concert hall literature.

Meanwhile concert courses, so called, had begun to grow into what has become a thriving business and a highly popular means of hearing at reasonable prices the world's best in individual and group musical talent. These brought into being the local middleman, the home-town impresario, and one of the first and best in the field was Mrs. Carlyle (Verna) Scott, who organized the University Artists Course in 1919 after staging a successful faculty show on the campus of the University of Minnesota.

The reign of Mrs. Scott, who was the wife of the university's music department chairman, was long and distinguished. She brought to town scores of the world's finest and most popular artists, booked the Chicago Civic Opera into the Minneapolis Auditorium for several seasons and later, at Northrop Auditorium, took over the management of the Minneapolis Symphony when it moved from its Eleventh Street location to the campus in 1930, and kept both campus and downtown concert halls copiously supplied with the stars the public loved or learned to love. She was chiefly instrumental in engaging two of the orchestra's most stimulating conductors, Eugene Ormandy in 1931 and Dimitri Mitropoulos in 1937.

At Mrs. Scott's resignation in 1938, Arthur Gaines resumed management of the orchestra (he had handled it from 1923 to 1930) and in 1944 James S. Lombard took charge of the highly successful University Artists Course, which has since proliferated into several well-attended concert series.

St. Paul's chief booker of musical talent over the years has been the Schubert Club. Its annual concert series is only one of a large docket of civic-music activities in which the club has helped deserving students, provided scholarships, brought music to hospitals and other institutions, and worked ceaselessly for better music more widely disseminated. The club is best known to lay concertgoers as the sharp-eyed seeker of outstanding talent on the rise; its record of snaring gifted musicians of oncoming fame before they are widely known is a brilliant one. It was the first to bring, for example, pianist Vladimir Horowitz to Minnesota, and those who heard him will never forget the excitement of that evening in the late 1920s when the floor of the old People's Church, where he played, shook during his furious crescendos and fortissimos.

Since 1939 the Women's Institute, sponsored by the *St. Paul Dispatch* and *Pioneer Press*, has helped to give the capital city full concert schedules; a similar sponsorship in Duluth by the *Herald* and *News-Tribune* has served that city well.

In Minneapolis the Thursday Musical, particularly in the era before the local impresarios entered the field, brought to the city many noted personalities and organizations, and occasionally sponsored opera and orchestra concerts. Later, under the thirty-six-year presidency of Mrs. H. S. Godfrey, its role as importer of outside talent gave way, in large part, to the promotion of local talent by making available a "show window" in biweekly concerts and offering scholarships to young musicians of promise.

The larger cities of Minnesota have not been the only benefi-
ciaries of the musical circuit riders whose routes are charted by
New York agencies. Many middle-sized towns of the region have
contracted for yearly concert series which bring them a wide variety
of performers, some of them booked by regional agencies.

Opera in Minnesota has had a long and checkered history,
marked by periods of surfeit and famine. Roughly from 1875 to
1895 was the period of greatest supply from the east, although as
early as 1865 an English opera troupe (Campbell and Castle's) had
staged a season of five light operas, including works of Donizetti
and Bellini, and Grau's Grand Opera Company had paid visits in
1867 and 1868.

Beginning in 1874, when the Adelaide Phillips company presented a full-scale production of Verdi's *Il Trovatore*, few seasons
lacked a full complement of opera repertoire, opera scenes, and
opera in concert. The great favorites were the Boston Ideals (later
reorganized as the Bostonians), and the adored Emma Abbott and
her companies, which kept coming back. The Hess Grand Opera
Company introduced Verdi's *Aïda* to the Twin Cities in the mid-
summer of 1890, and *Tristan und Isolde* made its bow in the
mid-nineties when Walter Damrosch's traveling Wagner Opera
Company came to Minneapolis at the behest of Anna Schoen-René,
at that time the city's most energetic entrepreneur.

From the early 1880s on, stars and casts from New York's
Metropolitan Opera House traveled under various company names
and managers, and the Twin Cities were their frequent hosts. After
the turn of the century the "Met" called at the Twin Cities in four
seasons during the first decade; this was followed by a long hiatus
until 1944, when a state-wide sponsors' group was set up to ar-
range a yearly season of four operas staged at Northrop Auditorium. These spring festivals draw patronage from an extensive
area, and they constitute the state's main, if meager, sustenance in
professional grand opera.

During the absence of the Metropolitan troupes, the frequent
visits of the San Carlo Company, and in 1929–30 two short seasons of the German Grand Opera Company starring Johanna Gad-

ski and devoted to Wagner repertoire (including the entire *Ring* cycle in four evenings), helped to keep the operatic pot simmering. Probably the most distinguished imported opera in the 1910–40 period was that of the Chicago Civic Opera which brought to St. Paul in 1922 Mary Garden as a tigerish Salome in the Richard Strauss opera, and staged some magnificent seasons during the subsequent decade in the Minneapolis and Northrop auditoriums. These later visits, among other attractions, brought Garden back in Alfano's *Resurrection* and Massenet's *Thaïs*, featured local premières of Montemezzi's *The Love of Three Kings* and Rimski-Korsakov's *Snow Maiden*, and (at Northrop) offered the memorable spectacle of blonde, imperious Maria Jeritza singing "Vissi d'arte" while lying on the floor in Puccini's *Tosca*.

With the avid interest in opera in Minnesota, these performances have merely whetted appetites, and numerous local efforts to stage this costly type of musical drama have been made. Among them was a Minneapolis Civic Opera that struggled and died in the 1930s; in the forties and fifties outdoor opera was presented in the unsatisfactory locale of Lake Harriet's north shore, a traffic-busy intersection with poor acoustics. Most enduring and successful of local enterprises has been the St. Paul Civic Opera Association, formed in 1932, which every season has provided a three-event series (with imported stars and musical and stage directors); in a quarter century it has traversed a wide gamut of grand and light opera and Broadway musical, all the way from Mozart to *Oklahoma!*

Concertized opera, occasionally with stylized sets and action, has been presented by the Minneapolis Symphony and the Duluth Symphony, and chamber opera has been offered on smaller stages at the Walker Art Center, the Minneapolis Institute of Arts, St. Paul's College of St. Catherine, and the University of Minnesota Theater. The scope of these endeavors is suggested by citing, at random, four noteworthy productions: Stravinsky's *L'histoire du soldat* (under Dimitri Mitropoulos at Hamline University in 1944), Monteverdi's *L'Orfeo*, Pergolesi's *La Serve Padrona*, Menotti's *The Medium* and *The Telephone*.

Chamber music in Minnesota has been a variable quantity, although there have been few seasons since 1890 when string quartets and small instrumental ensembles, in the Twin Cities at least, have not assembled and given concerts with fair regularity. These efforts have been motivated more by zeal to explore chamber music literature than by any hope of box-office booms.

The public taste for chamber music, never very marked, was slyly prodded as far back as the concerts in Harmonia Hall, where Frank Danz was wont to insert a short piece for string orchestra or string quartet into his programs. This novelty came to be an anticipated feature of his concerts. The string quartet in Danz's orchestra of the 1880s was made up of Fred Will, his concertmaster (who was also a theater orchestra leader), a Mr. Gangelhoff as second violinist, Danz himself as violinist, and Clarence Strachauer, a zealous and skillful chamber musician, as cellist.

Beginning in the 1890s string quartet music became a concert event in itself, and among the best known groups giving programs during that decade were St. Paul's Beethoven String Quartet and the ensembles organized by Claude Madden and Heinrich Hoevel. Stanchest proponent of the piano sonata in this period and later was the tireless and rather pedantic Hermann Emil Zoch, who ran up an awesome record of seventy-three sonata programs in the years between 1885 and 1913, all of them played from memory—an achievement not before or since duplicated by any other Minnesota pianist.

After the establishment of the Minneapolis Symphony in 1903, quartet playing became mostly the hobby, province, and responsibility of Symphony men, and we find concertmasters and string section leaders banding together for what has always been the intensest form of pleasure for musicians who like music. The names of the various groups shift about—the Minneapolis Symphony Quartet, the Minneapolis String Quartet, the Czerwonky String Quartet—and in 1914 we note the existence of a sponsoring organization, the Chamber Music Society of Minneapolis. Concertmasters generally played first violin—Fram Anton Korb, Richard Czerwonky, and later Joseph Shadwick and his successors were key figures in the cities' chamber music circles. Among the cellists were Carlo Fischer, Willy Lamping, and Cornelius Van Vliet.

With the coming in 1923 of Henri Verbrugghen as the second conductor of the Minneapolis Symphony, string quartet music, to which he was passionately devoted, took another spurt in Minneapolis. The Verbrugghen quartet (Verbrugghen and Jenny Cullen, violinists; David Nichols, violist; and James Messeas, cellist) was an experienced organization which had played in the British Isles and in Australia, where Verbrugghen had led the Sydney Conservatory Orchestra.

For a decade after the Verbrugghen regime, developments in chamber music in the Twin Cities were spotty, although concert courses then and earlier had hazarded a few programs by such distinguished groups as the Flonzaley, London, and Budapest quartets. Meanwhile the incidence of piano sonata and violin sonata programs, imported and local, was measurably on the increase.

In the 1950s, most chamber music of the stringed variety again emanated from the ranks of the Minneapolis Symphony. There have been, too, string and wind ensembles of varied instrumentation, and occasional reductions of the Minneapolis Symphony to chamber size in its regular programs. In 1958 five firmly established groups were providing music of chamber size and character, and mustering surprisingly large and loyal audiences: the Flor String Quartet, organized and led by Samuel Flor and playing regularly at Macalester College; the Trio da Camera, founded by Walter Targ, whose seat is the College of St. Catherine; the Variation String Quartet, headed by Kensley Rosen; and two sponsoring groups, the First Unitarian Society and the New Friends of Chamber Music, both of Minneapolis.

To be noted, also, is the entry of two art museums, the Minneapolis Institute of Arts and the Walker Art Center (the latter through its lay organization, the Center Arts Council), into the field of music sponsorship; by encouraging the production of chamber concerts and operas, they have provided an outlet for much unfamiliar material. James Aliferis and Gerard Samuel have taken the lead in the presentation of old and new music off the beaten paths.

The story of chamber music would not be complete without mentioning the provocative programs which the local chapter, now inactive, of the International Society for Contemporary Music staged, mostly during the tenure of composer Ernst Křenek at Hamline University in the 1940s.

Composers in Minnesota have been largely a migratory species, many of them born in the state and then moving away, others drawn to the area, usually by college and university music departments, and remaining as long as patience, opportunity, and income held out.

Some of Minnesota's nineteenth-century composers who were performed frequently in their time were Willard Patton who composed light operas, oratorios, and orchestral pieces, and who conducted the Philharmonic Club before Oberhoffer stepped in; Gustavus Johnson, who started a conservatory; E. O. Baldamus, A. M. Shuey (one of whose youthful indiscretions was the "Minne-ha-ha Falls Waltz"), William Rhys Herbert, and Ernest Lachmund of Minneapolis and Duluth. Of somewhat larger fame were Wesley LaViollette, native of St. James, whose *Penetrella* for string orchestra was played by the Minneapolis Symphony in 1929, and St. Paul-born Arthur Farwell, pupil of Humperdinck and one of the most notable composers and teachers to have claimed Minnesota as a birthplace.

Minnesota's list of part-time composers (few of this profession could or can subsist on composition alone) grows longer as we move into the twentieth century. Among the names linked with late nineteenth- and early twentieth-century styles are Donald Ferguson, the musicologist; Stanley R. Avery, for many years organist and choirmaster at St. Mark's Episcopal Church in Minneapolis; J. Victor Bergquist; Arthur Bergh; James A. Bliss; George Geist; Hamlin Hunt, long-time organist at Plymouth Congregational Church; and William Lindsay, a concert pianist who taught at the University of Minnesota. Orvis Ross of Rochester, piano pupil of Fannie Bloomfield Zeisler, has composed in many forms. In a class by himself was F. Melius Christiansen of Northfield, master of choral counterpoint.

A later group includes John Verrall, Ross Lee Finney, Everett Helm, and Marga Richter, now all Minnesota expatriates, and Gene Gutsche of White Bear Lake, who write in more advanced idioms. John J. Becker, aggressive advocate of dissonance, was for a time at St. Thomas Academy in St. Paul. The newer names, all of them associated with the University of Minnesota, are James Aliferis, Earl George, Paul Fetler, Lothar Klein, and Wayne Peterson. Vincent Carpenter at Macalester and Russell G. Harris at Hamline lead the academic contingent in St. Paul. Among the choral composers must be mentioned Olaf C. and Paul J. Christiansen, C. Wesley Anderson, Arthur B. Jennings, Leland B. Sateren, Peter Tkach, Paul Manz, Frederick Wick, and Ralph Williams.

One of the seminal forces in composition in Minnesota, from 1942 to 1948, was Ernst Křenek, the Czech-Austrian composer of *Jonny Spielt Auf* who since composing that jazz opera has adopted the twelve-tone method. He became dean of Hamline's fine arts department and not only exerted an influence on the Minneapolis Symphony's programming but developed on the St. Paul campus a small coterie of creative pupils.

All the Minneapolis Symphony conductors have dabbled to a varying extent in composition or transcriptions, as most conductors do. Emil Oberhoffer wrote two works played by the orchestra, "Overture Romantique" and "Americana," a festival march of homage. Henri Verbrugghen is probably best remembered for his little souvenir from the antipodes, "Waiata Poi," a Maori song composed by Alfred Hill and orchestrated by the conductor. One of his own works was a "Fantasia on British Sea Songs." Except for some arrangements, Eugene Ormandy and Dimitri Mitropoulos did little composition — none that was publicly audible at least — although the latter as a youth had written an opera, *Soeur Beatrice*, based on a Maeterlinck play. The fifth conductor, Antal Dorati, has been more active in this field. His arrangements for ballet, *Bluebeard* and *Helen of Troy*, using the music of Offenbach, and *Graduation Ball*, to the music of Johann Strauss, are widely known, and more recently he has composed a cello concerto, a work for chorus and orchestra, *The Way of the Cross*, and some song settings.

The role of educators' organizations and musical clubwomen in holding clinics, sponsoring contests, and offering scholarships has increased vastly in importance in recent years. Among the most active in the club field has been the Minnesota Federation of Music Clubs, and in the professional realm the Minnesota Music Educators' Association, the state units of the Music Teachers' National Association and the American String Teachers' Association, and the Minnesota Public School Music League.

The history of jazz in Minnesota merits more than the brief synopsis we must give it. This vital and spontaneous musical expression began to make itself felt in the early 1920s, mostly in the Twin Cities area. At the start it was music on the "wrong side of the tracks," a maverick form whose detractors scorned it as a vulgar outgrowth of what was considered equally vulgar ragtime. It survived the contempt of the genteel (including those whose tastes had been wholly conditioned in the concert hall) and grew in the esteem of a younger generation that accepted it avidly and of professionals who recognized its significance as a viable, American-rooted music.

The concert-going laity had its first encounter with jazz, in a hybrid and polished form, when Paul Whiteman visited the Twin Cities in 1925 and climaxed his program with the Gershwin *Rhapsody in Blue*. Few in the audience who heard his big virtuoso orchestra were aware, however, of a humbler and genuine jazz played in the smoky interiors of speakeasies, and later bars and roadhouses, by small bands improvising (by ear) on popular melodies — cornet, clarinet, and trombone in the extempore roles, drums, piano, string bass, and guitar or banjo supplying the "beat." Student groups at the University of Minnesota and on other campuses embraced enthusiastically the music which came to be known as Dixieland. The popularity of Dixieland dimmed in the early thirties, but an upturn of interest came late in that decade when Mitch's (a tavern in Mendota) became a rallying ground for performers and listeners. The original New Orleans influence was reinforced by Chicago musicians venturing northwestward.

At Mitch's, Paul (Doc) Evans, who had earlier studied piano and played saxophone, began to attract favorable notice by his clear-cut, driving cornet style, and he has become the region's outstanding interpreter, nationally known, of the "pure" Dixieland style, in recent years building up a large group of aficionados in outdoor summer concerts at Walker Art Center.

Meanwhile the jazz idiom had undergone the conceptual and stylistic changes of swing and bop to attain, after World War II, a new and "cool" form known as progressive or modern, a subtler, more cerebral patterning developed mainly in New York and California. This sophisticated trend attracted more conservatory-trained musicians than its precursors and involved more composed-on-paper music together with a wider range of instrumentation permitting new tone colors drawn from classical music. Among the state's leading practitioners of this style are Bob Davis and the German-born and -trained Herb Pilhofer, with such creative player-improvisers as the flutist Dave Karr contributing quality and inventiveness to the new and still-developing idiom.

Music in Minnesota in its manifold aspects is a thriving and progressive institution. In performance, which draws the lay public whose function is to listen, to enjoy an enriching experience, and to support; in the skills of executants developed in music schools and colleges and countless studios; in the do-it-yourself activities of nonprofessional musicians, young and old, who sing in choirs and play in orchestras; in the accelerating spread of music appreciation in formal education and over radio and television—in all the manifestations of this art, business, and entertainment, Minnesota has a long-time investment and a warm, vigorous, and continuing interest.

꒦꒷

Writing of the theater's first century in Minnesota tends to be a nostalgic exercise of recalling the abundant past from a bleak perch in the deprived present. The "road," which started up the

Mississippi River in the 1850s and overland in the 1860s when rails first reached the Twin Cities, bore a bustling caravan of theatrical riches for seventy-five years and a meager and dwindling cargo for the twenty-five that followed.

Traveling actors and companies once made Minnesota's stages a focus of social and cultural interests. Here Shakespeare, Boucicault's thrillers, Edwin Booth, and *Uncle Tom's Cabin* all had their turn in enthralling, delighting, and sometimes chafing a public which had few other diversions. These visitors certainly do not make up the whole panorama of the theater in Minnesota, and their declining number has had compensation in the rise of a more vigorous and responsible local theater, as we shall see. But the dominant and most dramatic element of our chronicle is inescapably the traveling theater, with its helpmate (and occasional rival) the resident stock company that provided regular repertory, over varying periods, in the nineteenth and early twentieth century.

Appropriately enough, Minnesota's centennial marks roughly a century of theatrical activity in the state, although a prologue of sorts was played in territorial days as far back as 1851, in pioneer St. Paul, and for three prior decades in amateur theatricals at Fort Snelling.

It seems probable that soldiers quartered at the Fort in the 1820s, encircled by wilderness and reacting against the boredom of garrison life, staged the first dramatic production in Minnesota-to-be. Their performance in the winter of 1821–22 of Kotzebue's melodrama of Peru, *Pizarro*, is the earliest recorded dramatic presentation in Minnesota, known to us through the recollections of Joseph R. Brown, later editor of the *Henderson Democrat*, who portrayed Elvira in borrowed feminine garb. Eventually the soldiers even traveled with their theatricals to make appearances in St. Paul after it took on the semblance of a village in the early fifties.

To visualize the earliest theater in Minnesota we must forget gilded prosceniums, plush seats, orchestra pits, and stages and imagine instead wooden frame buildings with slightly raised platforms at one end of upstairs halls, over saloons or stores. Seats were benches. Illumination was by oil and kerosene lamps.

To these crude halls came the first troupes in the 1850s, arriving by river steamer in St. Paul, the head of navigation, from as far off as New Orleans. Pioneer of them all was a company known as Placide's Varieties, which on August 12, 1851, gave the first professional performance in Minnesota, starring George Holland, a noted eccentric comedian who managed the troupe. For some years St. Paul, which in the early fifties had a population of about 1,000, was chief beneficiary of the talents of roving players who could act, sing, strum guitars, dance, and even do an acrobatic turn or walk a tight wire. The smaller Minneapolis and St. Anthony to the west, beyond river navigation, had to wait until the summer of 1857 before a theatrical company—Sallie St. Clair's Varieties—visited them; they then relapsed into another nine years of theaterlessness, a period during which St. Paul saw no fewer than 450 productions.

Traveling companies at this time were loosely knit organizations clustered about a star-manager, male or female; often filled with performers picked up en route or locally, they were rarely first-rate in quality and offered miscellaneous fare. Theatrical seasons in the Twin Cities were just the reverse of what they later became —the warm months rather than the cold ones, May to October, while the river was open. After the freezeup, problems of heating halls made play-giving and playgoing a numbing and nonprofit enterprise. Later, theaters in the cities were heated in the winter, but the halls in neighboring towns were not, and troupes that needed to perform regularly on tour to make ends meet (and they all did) could not afford to get snowbound in northern climes. It was not until 1867 that a winter company was started in St. Paul.

Touring groups usually leased a hall and played their repertoire as long as they had a paying audience, their members becoming temporary residents and familiar figures in town. Then they pulled out for the next stop, piecing out their tour with one- or two-night stands along the way. Often they would collapse and disperse; often the star or manager would withhold wages or, worse yet, disappear with the receipts. On the fringes of the theatrical fraternity was that dogged and forlorn tribe that plied the muddy or dusty roads to smaller hamlets by buggy or wagon, putting up tents in vacant lots, staging minstrel or Uncle Tom shows, or singing and selling medicinal oil under flares on street corners.

A Minnesota circuit was built up in time, and such centers as Stillwater, Red Wing, Winona and other river towns, Duluth, Moorhead, St. Cloud, Wadena, Crookston, and Brainerd, together with smaller towns nearer the big cities, all welcomed the touring mummers as opera houses and better halls sprang up. The important fact is that the national boom in traveling theater came at precisely the time when Minnesota could take full advantage of it. The new railroads which provided access to the state and its own rapidly growing population and prosperity helped to make Minnesota promising terrain for the stars and producers who were then discovering inland America. By 1885, Minnesota had forty-seven towns with theaters housing plays and variety shows.

But even before the railroads St. Paul residents, as we have noted, were offered a generous sampling of itinerant entertainment. Placide's Varieties from New Orleans, which had offered the typical fare of the day—farces, musical skits, melodramas, and diverse novelties—was followed in 1852 by Langrishe and Atwater's Theatrical Corps, a regional troupe advertising "all the best in Tragedies, Comedies, Operas, Farces, Burlesques, etc., etc." The "best" included plays now dated and gone to limbo—Kotzebue's *The Stranger*, Bulwer-Lytton's *The Lady of Lyons* (which was a durable play, however: its last Minneapolis appearance was in 1905), and Knowles' *William Tell*.

In 1854 St. Paul had its first taste of Shakespeare. Just a taste it was, and curiously flavored, for *Hamlet* was cut to two scenes, *Richard III* was played by a cast of six, and both title roles were taken by an actress, Charlotte Crampton. Many actresses then and later essayed male Shakespearean roles (reversing the Elizabethan custom of boys in female parts). Twenty years after Miss Crampton, Susan Denin was to be chided by critics for her overly plump Romeo, as was Nelly Boyd for forgetting she was a lady who ought to give up bifurcated garb. (Roles were sometimes shifted about: Miss Boyd, curiously enough, played Juliet to Miss Denin's Romeo.)

From then on the practice of women taking heroes' roles diminished, although as late as 1882 Anna Dickinson appeared as Hamlet, arousing more mirth than admiration.

More effective, in that first decade, were C. W. Couldock, a tragedian of repute, in *Othello* and other Shakespeare repertory; a first *Camille* in 1856; and the skilled Mr. and Mrs. J. W. Wallack as Macbeth and his blood-stained lady.

The 1850s also witnessed a brave attempt at local theater management in St. Paul, and the first effort to assemble a resident company with occasional visiting stars. Henry Van Liew built the town's first opera house at a cost of $750 and persevered for a time against mounting odds, but finally gave up and left town after his barn-like structure burned down in 1859. Theaters then and for decades to come burned with discouraging regularity, and not the least hazard of theatergoing was the danger of fire in highly combustible buildings.

St. Paul in the fifties and sixties was a mecca for home seekers, fortune hunters, and those lured by its much publicized healthful climate; its boom was interrupted only by the 1857 panic and the Civil War. A crowded theatrical calendar developed among its residents the beginnings of what eventually became a discriminating palate for dramatic goods. But across the river Minneapolis and St. Anthony remained for fifteen years backward and "backwoods." Their largely Yankee population gave them a reputation for a puritan hostility toward the theater which, together with their inaccessibility, put them out of bounds for nervous thespians. A St. Anthony pastor in 1857 inveighed against the sinful institution on the grounds that it did violence to "the moral feelings and virtue of the audience" and that "the men and women who appear on the stage are usually persons of bad character."

The fact that certain performers' addiction to drink made them bungle lines or even miss or cause cancellation of a performance seemed to confirm the low opinion of the theater held by its critics. The issue of the stage's wickedness was debated from time to time in newspaper columns, its "edifying influence" defended, and its corrupting habits—late hours, liquor, and loose morals—

deplored. The alcoholic defections of the popular comedian John Dillon brought sharp criticism from the press of this "common drunkard" without appreciably lessening the public's fondness for him. Harry Duncan's "indisposition" which caused his absence from the cast of *Mary Stuart* in 1868 drew a caustic suggestion from the *St. Paul Daily Press*: "He should be sent to an asylum."

But players were not the sole target of the moralists. Later, in 1873, the *Minneapolis Tribune* found that Joseph Jefferson's starring play, *Rip Van Winkle*, conveyed an objectionable message by making Rip, after his twenty years' slumber, return thirstily to the bottle as soon as possible after waking up. "The lesson of the whole thing is bad," it concluded. Even Richard Brinsley Sheridan was called to account. *The School for Scandal*, in 1882, was frowned upon because "its plots and counterplots all relate to the relations between sexes."

The quality of Twin Cities dramatic fare showed some improvement after the hiatus caused by the Civil War. The Templeton Company from the south, with the later famous Fay Templeton a toddling baby at the first of its many engagements, was described as an old-fashioned stock company "of rare excellence." Its performance of Dumas' *Camille*, a play apt to offend the genteel, was deemed acceptable because of the "extreme delicacy" with which it was handled.

The Macfarland Consolidation, which came upriver for summer seasons, shared with Charles Plunkett, a Shakespearean specialist, most of the entertainment responsibilities in the Twin Cities in the late sixties. Macfarland was the first to play in the new St. Paul Opera House, and he introduced the bewitching singer-actress Emilie Melville, who was equally popular in *Fanchon, the Cricket* (a play based on a George Sand novel) and in Donizetti's light opera *The Daughter of the Regiment*. Actor-manager Plunkett, an Englishman who had played Othello to Couldock's Iago in New York's Old Bowery Theater, brought a wide repertoire ranging from *The Merchant of Venice* to *Ten Nights in a Bar Room*. His productions were frequent in the Twin Cities in the sixties, but his acting lost favor during the later years of his stay; he weighed nearly 300 pounds and the asthma he suffered from made him puff and wheeze through his lines. In the next (and more sophisticated) decade he hied to "the sticks," where the provincialism of his performances was less noticed and criticized. He usually climaxed his seasons with his favorite role of Othello.

All was not Shakespeare, melodrama, and sentiment in those days. The famous dance spectacle which had caused a sensation in the east, *The Black Crook*, was presented in 1867 as St. Paul's first "leg show," but there was some difficulty in assembling enough of that anatomical equipment. Producer Macfarland advertised for twenty-five young ladies to learn the ballet formations. As it turned out, there was little dancing to be described as such, although the local girls showed good teamwork in the play's climactic march of the Amazons.

The theater in that period was committed, above all, to diversity, not only in repertoire which would find a single company swinging from *Hamlet* to farce and moral drama but in the composition of a single evening's fare. Often a performance would be preceded by orchestral pieces or vocal solos; a much-applauded actor might respond to an encore with a dramatic reading. Then again, three plays, necessarily short, might be staged in one evening.

Multiple roles were a test of virtuosity and keenly appreciated; comedian George Holland played as many as six characters in one play, displaying the same kind of cleverness as that shown by the quick-change artists of later vaudeville. In 1867 Mollie Williams ran up the same score in *A Day in Paris*.

A curiosity of the period, too, was the so-called equestrian actor or actress in what were called equestrian dramas or "horse operas," whose definition differed from the much later one designating western drama or films. Bob Miles was among the first of these horseback actors, and later Kate Fisher emulated the famous Adah Isaacs Menken in the melodrama *Mazeppa* (based on Byron's poem) wherein that shapely star, in flesh-colored tights, was strapped to the back of a galloping steed. Miss Fisher was even more of a specialist than Miss Menken; she played all her roles astride Wonder, her trained horse. Wonder must have been well trained indeed, for he had to mount two flights of stairs to the Pence Opera House stage for every performance.

Minstrel shows had a long heyday, and one of the early and prominent figures in minstrel history—Dan Emmett, author of the song *Dixie*—had visited St. Paul in the late fifties. Panoramas depicting battles (Gettysburg, the Monitor and Merrimac) and scenes from foreign lands claimed a good share of public attention in the early years of the state.

One of the serious malaises of the peripatetic theater in its first three decades was a "star system" which found prominent actors and actresses surrounded by inferior casts—a situation which was to prevail, under different circumstances, well into the twentieth century. From the fifties through the seventies, the great stars often traveled alone, depending on stock companies or semipermanent resident troupes to make up their supporting casts—much as violinists and pianists always have depended on local orchestras for concerto interpretations. Newspaper comment time and again refers to the brilliance of a star's performance in a shoddy setting of supporting talent.

A golden age of theater in Minnesota had its beginnings in this period, however. The state was to welcome some of the finest performing artists of the late nineteenth century and the pick of the plays from New York and other producing centers.

Among the better plays were George H. Boker's poetic tragedy *Francesca da Rimini*, Steele MacKaye's domestic drama *Hazel Kirke*, James A. Herne's melodrama *Hearts of Oak*, and William Gillette's Civil War spy story *Held by the Enemy*. Among the great popular successes of the time, each of them a starring vehicle, were *Davy Crockett*, *Rip Van Winkle*, and *The Two Orphans*, the latter a pathetic melodrama of French extraction which returned again and again. There were countless performances of *Camille* and of Augustin Daly's *Under the Gaslight*, which had a sensational climax showing a train speeding toward a male victim tied to the railroad track. Boucicault's *Streets of New York* had thrills, too, in its lurid and realistic panorama of city life. Tom Taylor's *The Ticket-of-Leave Man* introduced an infallible detective—Hawkshaw—long before Conan Doyle invented Sherlock Holmes. The century's best seller, *Uncle Tom's Cabin*, was dramatized in countless versions. This deteriorated into a species of sideshow in which the bloodhounds earned bigger billing than the actors.

Laura Keene was well past her peak when she first came to Minneapolis in 1870, but her name was still glamorous enough to make her a big "draw." Among her offerings was another play by Tom Taylor, *Our American Cousin*, in which she had made her first success twelve years before with Joseph Jefferson and Edward A. Sothern.

Davy Crockett was to make Frank Mayo virtually a one-role actor until the year of his death, 1896, just as Joseph Jefferson was perennially Rip Van Winkle, Maggie Mitchell an everlasting Fanchon, and James O'Neill (father of playwright Eugene O'Neill) a tireless and ever-touring Count of Monte Cristo. But Mayo first appeared in the Twin Cities in *Hamlet, Macbeth*, and *Richard III* (making the mistake of presenting them on three hot and ill-attended July evenings), and he did not bring his Tennessee trapper to town until four years later, in 1875.

Lawrence Barrett's repertoire of Shakespeare and Bulwer-Lytton's *Richelieu* was critically embraced but publicly shunned. In 1872 he had been among the first to organize his own company as a guaranty of good ensemble. His productions had quality and probably a heavy payroll, for the admission prices he charged were higher than most people wanted to pay. But no such misfortune befell the appearances of Lotta (born Charlotte) Crabtree, rapturously described as the "pet and pride of California" and "100 pounds of frolic," who drew capacity audiences for her three plays, *Zip, The Little Detective*, and *Little Nell*.

The seventies were further marked by the notable combination of Barrett and E. L. Davenport in *Julius Caesar*, and the "divinely tall, divinely fair" Mary Anderson making her Minnesota bow only five months after her conquest of New York. She spoke inaudibly but was praised for a figure described as "superbly classical." Maggie Mitchell's Fanchon — "ingenuous, passionate, wild" — drew poorly in Minneapolis and enthusiastically in St. Paul, where the only hint of detraction was a reviewer's comment on her excessive kittenishness: "It would be a relief if she remained quiet, if only for a moment." The Fifth Avenue Company of Augustin Daly, who was one of the producing geniuses of the period and a prolific playwright, impressed critics by the high average level of its acting, unmarred by the "miserable supes" usually seen in troupes from the east. Kate Claxton brought back the play she was to tour for twenty years, *The Two Orphans* aforementioned, in which she played blind Louise. On a lighter note, Tony Pastor's variety troupe, in 1875, featured a "flip-flap fandango" and staged, incredibly, *Venus and Adonis* on velocipedes. The Worrell Sisters' company offered guitar duets, trapeze performances, and clog dancing.

Elaborate scenic effects and various simulated perils and disasters more and more concerned play producers. In Minneapolis much of the credit for the public's ever growing fascination with the theater went to a scene painter and designer, Peter Clausen. It was he who created with uncanny effect the breaking up of polar ice in a play called *Sea of Ice*, where a ship came to the rescue of characters facing death from starvation and freezing while a blazing aurora borealis filled the arctic sky. Clausen outdid himself in 1878 for a production of *The Streets of New York*, wherein he whipped up a snowstorm in Union Square, showed streetcars passing to and fro, and capped his efforts in a frightening fire scene with flame and smoke and an actual—and chugging—fire engine. At the climax of all this, related a reviewer, the hero "rushes through a door, ascends to the second floor, and saves the valued receipt for $100,000, a moment later appearing at a second-story window and jumping to the ground."

Clausen and his mastery of scenic illusion contributed much to the success of an important development in Minneapolis' theater annals—the founding by John Murray of a high-grade stock company, the Murray-Cartland Company. The quality of its productions at the Pence Opera House had the double result of introducing a healthy rivalry with a competing playhouse, the Academy of Music, and of discouraging visits by many mediocre traveling troupes, which hesitated to risk comparisons. The company also developed the city's first "matinee idol," Frederick Bryton, a handsome and versatile actor who had a loyal following. Active from 1878 to 1883, John Murray built up a large repertoire, changing the bill nearly every night and taking time out to tour the state.

The value of a resident stock company was not lost on St. Paul, for the eighties saw the rise (and customary decline) of two worthy enterprises striving to strike roots in the community. Col. J. H. Wood came from Detroit in 1882 and transformed a vacant meatpacking house into a "neat little theater" whose offerings were better than anyone had reason to expect. Wood soon attracted standing-room-only attendance but suffered the inevitable fire and sold his interests in 1883. After five years the People's Stock Company, a more ambitious undertaking which had a roster of no fewer than thirty-seven players, got under way but lasted no longer than its predecessor, despite an auspicious start and performances of above-average quality.

In the eighties, the touring stars and companies came in ever increasing numbers to fill the gaps left by the unstable resident companies. Edwin Booth, the century's great Hamlet, appeared first in Minneapolis in 1882, rather late in his career, and returned to the cities in 1886 (with Lawrence Barrett) and again in 1888. He was in his middle fifties by this time (he died in 1893) and critics noted his advancing years and increased melancholy of demeanor, his "quiet and intense" mode of acting in contrast to the more animated style of Barrett.

Tommaso Salvini from Italy, big-voiced, imposing, of fiery temperament, spoke Italian with English-speaking casts, a circumstance that combined with high ticket prices (at $2) to make his audiences small. Also from Italy on her farewell tour came Adelaide Ristori, a Lady Macbeth and Medea in the grand style; from Belgium, the famous Rhea; from Bohemia, Fanny Janauschek. Two memorable Camilles, from Poland and France, had critics and public comparing the "spirituelle" Helena Modjeska with the more passionate Sarah Bernhardt—the first "more beautiful and winning," the latter "lithe and willowy."

Comparison, too, was made between these foreign tragediennes and their American counterparts, Clara Morris, whose attacks of neuralgia protracted her local performance of *Camille* until midnight, and the tall and striking Fanny Davenport, who had a lighter side as seen in *As You Like It* and *The School for Scandal.*

Tragedy, at this time, was changing its emphasis. The long-prevailing dominance of male actors was gradually giving way to an insistent female intrusion. The tragic mask was acquiring a tear as the accent changed from masculine to feminine, from the heroic to the pathetic. A new phenomenon, the emotional actress, a Camille but rarely a Lady Macbeth, was to weep and wring her hands well into the twentieth century.

Concurrent with this trend was the gradual expansion of melodrama into melodramatic spectacle, with all kinds of ingenious stage effects to enhance realism, brought to perfection in the eighties. This was a matter largely of mechanical device and scenic illusion to arouse the wonderment of spectators. At the same time, a deeper realism in the treatment of human character and a keener observation of real life were beginning to make their mark on the American stage. The Harrigan and Hart shows depicted New York types (Irish- and German-Americans, and Negroes) who had rarely before been portrayed on the stage, and Charles Hoyt's farcical comedies were peopled with city and village folk broadly drawn.

During the eighties and toward 1900, what might be called the proto-musical comedy slowly took form as the earlier double bills were replaced by full-length musical farce comedies, related to *opéra bouffe* and catering to the taste developed by the invasion of comic opera initiated by Gilbert and Sullivan's *H. M. S. Pinafore* in the late seventies. Lower-browed appeal had been exerted by female minstrels, cancan dancers, and a procession of girl shows offering everything from "living art statues" and prancing British blondes to Mlle. Sidonia's Frisky French Favorites.

The latter represented the trend that grew into modern burlesque, but the song-and-dance show with a plot framework, usually flimsy, increased in favor and frequency and in the middle nineties took on the form that would be applied and adapted for some four decades to come. An early example was Charles Hoyt's *A Trip to Chinatown* with its popular song "The Bowery! the Bowery! . . . I'll never go there any more," which came to the Twin Cities in 1890, 1894, and 1908. Nearer still to the modern musical comedy was *A Gaiety Girl*, a British import, first produced in 1893 and reaching the Twin Cities belatedly in 1902.

The nineties in Minnesota and particularly in the Twin Cities were a time of accelerated change and waxing fortunes in the theater, as in the field of concert and opera, slowed only temporarily by the 1893 panic. Old playhouses were giving way to new ones, a new entrepreneur—L. N. Scott— had entered the scene to become the outstanding theater manager for nearly thirty-five years in Minneapolis, St. Paul, and Duluth, and around the turn of the century more people were seeing more plays than at any other time before or since.

Big business methods made their first impress during the decade, materializing in the so-called Theatrical Syndicate. Six men including Marc Klaw and Abraham Erlanger organized this central agency in New York and succeeded soon in creating a monopoly which gained control of most of the theaters in America. Scott, who had taken a hand in the early planning for the syndicate, became its Minnesota representative. The syndicate held despotic sway over bookings and playhouses until another powerful combine, the Shubert Brothers, began to dislodge it in the first decade of the new century by building a network of its own theaters, including the two Shubert theaters in Minneapolis and St. Paul.

Among many local managers and a number of stars there was resistance to the syndicate, most of it futile, but the public was no loser in the innumerable plays and players that came to the Metropolitan Opera houses of the Twin Cities during Scott's long tenure. These and the other downtown theaters rarely had a "dark" night. In Minneapolis, three houses were in almost continuous operation —the Metropolitan (which opened in 1894 as the People's Theater), the Bijou, and the Lyceum (the earlier theater by that name, on Hennepin Avenue near Seventh Street). The lavish Grand Opera House on Sixth Street had given up the ghost with the Metropoli-

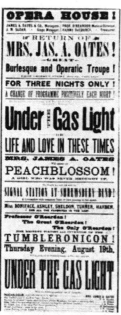

An early handbill

The Minneapolis Metropolitan
Theater (1898)

The Lyceum Theater, Duluth (1910)

tan's entry, and the ancient Pence faded out as the Bijou became the chief lower loop theater. In St. Paul the two leading legitimate theaters, the Grand Opera House and the Metropolitan Opera House, had the lights on most nights of the year.

Jacob Litt of Milwaukee had taken over the Bijou in 1889 and started a long occupancy of that Washington Avenue playhouse. In 1892 he introduced a play, *In Old Kentucky*, which for eighteen years was to be the standard fall opener, an annual attraction for State Fair visitors. This melodrama of the old south, by Charles T. Dazey, ranked second only to *Uncle Tom's Cabin* in number of performances; in three years' time it had already made a reported $25,000 for its backer Litt. A clue to the appeal of this sure-fire hit can be found in the motto (slightly misquoted) that was printed on every program: "True hearts are more than coronets, and simple faith than Norman blood." Each evening, before the performance, a ragtime concert was given by a "pickaninny band," and in addition to these pickaninnies were advertised the "breezy Kentucky colonel, the delightful mountain lass, and Queen Bess, the Kentucky thoroughbred." Horses were still popular, despite the invasion of bloodhounds in the "Uncle Tom shows." The great horse show of the period was *Ben Hur*, and the better productions had eight steeds, all galloping on treadmills.

The Bijou took care of the popular taste and the "B" attractions, the Lyceum (which led a rather checkered career) housed an assortment of productions, good, bad, and indifferent, while the Metropolitan quickly took rank as the class house of the city.

In Duluth the Lyceum and later the Orpheum were ports of call for plays and variety that made the city a lively show town until the twenties, after which, as elsewhere, a decline set in.

The calendar of shows reaching the Twin Cities in the years around the turn of the century—many of them also performed in other towns of the state—offered a plenitude that stirs envy in today's theater addict as he peruses it a half century later. To pick a normally busy month at random, October of 1906, we find ten plays at the Metropolitan in 38 performances, five at the Lyceum in 40 performances, and another five at the Bijou in 40 performances—a total of twenty plays in 188 performances in thirty-one days.

Not all these plays, of course, were masterpieces, but they included Charles Klein's *The Lion and the Mouse*, George M. Cohan in his *Forty-Five Minutes from Broadway*, James O'Neill in *Monte Cristo*, Winston Churchill's *The Crisis*, and Montgomery and Stone in the musical comedy based on L. Frank Baum's *The Wizard of Oz*.

Picking an earlier year, 1898, we may summarize its highlights: five light opera companies, four stock companies (Neill, McKee Rankin, and Henderson companies in the summer, Woodward in the winter), Richard Mansfield in *Beau Brummel* and *Dr. Jekyll and Mr. Hyde*, Thomas Keene in seven nights of Shakespeare, Chauncey Olcott in an Irish play, and vaudeville and minstrels at the Bijou and Metropolitan.

The names of American playwrights exploring a new and vigorous vein of realism began to appear on the playbills: Clyde Fitch, Augustus Thomas, Eugene Walter, William Vaughn Moody, Edward Sheldon, George H. Broadhurst, Rachel Crothers; and theatergoers were offered "problem plays," usually tinged with melodrama. The works of foreign dramatists were also seen: Pinero, Barrie, Wilde and Shaw, Sudermann and Ibsen, Rostand and Sardou. Ibsen, after shocking a St. Paul reviewer by exhibiting a housewife who not only left her husband but deserted her children, fared much better later, particularly in Minneapolis where a large Norwegian population may have had some effect in stimulating praise for a Norwegian genius. If Ibsen was idolized, Shaw was often as not raked over the coals for subversive thinking and, among other things, for lacking proper respect for women in general and prospective mothers in particular.

Sunday performances in theaters were bitterly opposed in the early nineties but agitation against them lessened toward the close of the decade. The panic of 1893 caused a decline in attendance for a time, and efforts were made to lure theatergoers by gifts of souvenir spoons, photographs of players, bouquets of flowers, and even tons of coal.

L. N. Scott   Dick Ferris

The turn of the century heard the birth cries of two entertainment mediums which were to compete with the playhouses, one in fraternal rivalry for about a quarter century, the other for a longer period and with far more lethal effects. Vaudeville was an outgrowth of variety and had as long an ancestry as the theater itself; the difference now was that theaters were built specifically for vaudeville which had been organized in nation-wide circuits. The movies made their first appearance in nickelodeons—usually remodeled stores—and for a time were nothing more than a cheap novelty which had "no future."

Most interesting of the stock ventures in the 1900–10 period was Dick Ferris' occupancy of the Lyceum, a theater which had prospered only fitfully. A flamboyant man about town with a gift for promotion, Ferris, with his wife, Grace Hayward, started in 1902 a three-year tenancy of the house and kept it supplied with plays of middling merit. Ferris managed, directed, and frequently took part in the plays, which ranged indiscriminately from Hall Caine's *The Christian* to *Ten Nights in a Barroom*, with Miss Hayward as his leading lady. In time he acquired a fond and sizable following, largely female at the matinees, but he was more showman than artist. His second wife, Florence Stone, became his star in 1904–5 and continued to play with him after he left the Lyceum for a series of summer seasons at the Metropolitan continuing through 1909. Ferris' last appearance on a Minneapolis stage was in 1915, when A. G. Bainbridge, Jr., engaged Miss Stone for his stock company at the new Sam S. Shubert theater and took Ferris into the cast for two weeks.

"Buzz" Bainbridge was an energetic and boldly imaginative promoter who as a youth had been a circus press representative and later managed a dramatic stock company in Duluth. He became Minnesota's most enterprising and successful manager-producer in the first third of the century, and his major accomplishment was that of founding and maintaining the longest-lived stock company in the history of the state, and probably of the country as well. The Bainbridge Players, as the company was usually called, prospered for an unbroken two decades of seasons, from 1912 to 1933. In the latter year, Bainbridge was elected mayor of Minneapolis.

Bainbridge was keenly aware of two essentials for keeping a stock company solvent — he knew how to pick his casts and stars, and he had a gift for sustaining theatergoers' personal interest in his "acting family." His first selection of stars, Lee Baker and Edith Evelyn, the latter Richard Mansfield's former leading lady, initiated a successful series of plays that instilled in the townspeople a weekly habit of attending the Shubert. He signed up Florence Roberts and cast her in such plays as Sardou's *Madame Sans-Gêne* and Daudet's *Sapho*. Another of his early standbys was Louise Farnum. Averill Harris proved a versatile leading man. The gifted Florence Stone, who soon eclipsed her husband Dick Ferris, could in one week give verisimilitude and conviction to Rebecca (of Sunnybrook Farm) and in the next to a sultry Cleopatra. She was to prove one of the pillars of the troupe, and a long-continuing favorite with playgoers.

Bainbridge's most important choice of stars, however, was blithe and winsome Marie Gale, a former dramatics school pupil who, after shyly auditioning at a theater tryout, entered the company in 1914 as an "extra." Her first performance was in the part of Milk in Maeterlinck's *The Bluebird*. Seven years later she had risen to

Buzz Bainbridge   Marie Gale

Light, the leading role of that allegory; in the interval she had become Bainbridge's bride, taken on increasingly important assignments, and eventually had her name in capitals in the program.

Miss Gale became the darling of the Shubert's clientele and she played an immense number and variety of parts, from cheerful moppets like Pollyanna to sinful ladies like Sadie Thompson in *Rain*. She "retired" from time to time but always came back to fanfares of publicity and gleeful welcomes from her doting public. Before she quit the stage for good she was to play more than 200 roles.

Meanwhile Bainbridge worked out yearly schedules which most of the time kept his customers amused, some of the time inspired them, and once in a while even educated them. He offered modern and controversial plays; he made frequent bows to Ibsen and Shaw and one to Andreyev (in *He Who Gets Slapped*); he staged *Romeo and Juliet* in 1927. He played Barrie (*What Every Woman Knows* and *The Little Minister*), and St. John Ervine (*John Ferguson* and *Jane Clegg*). He introduced two original plays by William J. McNally, a Minneapolis drama critic whose *Prelude to Exile* was later seen in New York in a Theatre Guild production. He produced Benavente's *The Passion Flower* with Virginia Safford, social leader and future journalist, in the leading role. He gave the public what it wanted and frequently what it ought to have.

A typical season was that of 1923–24 when he offered forty plays, mostly comedies but including six of substantial merit, some in their local premières — Eugene O'Neill's *Beyond the Horizon* and *Anna Christie*, Molnar's *Liliom*, Pinero's *The Second Mrs. Tanqueray*, Owen Davis' *Icebound*, and Sudermann's *Magda*. During the season he had engaged the dynamic Florence Reed for seven weeks, inaugurating a new guest star policy which was to bring to the city, in the next few years, Mrs. Leslie Carter, Blanche Ring, Edith Taliaferro, Clara Kimball Young, Martha Hedman, Lillian Foster, Marjorie Rambeau, and Alice Brady. At the same time the Shubert Players sent several of their own members to Broadway: Victor Jory, Gladys George, and Jean Dixon were among the graduates. Other "regulars" of the company in the twenties were Johnny Dilson, Joseph and Helen De Stefani, Guy Usher, Dorrit Kelton, and Ruth Lee.

Stock, popular in Minneapolis, never had much luck or long continuity in St. Paul. In that city the Shubert housed various troupes from 1910 until the mid-thirties, when it became a movie theater, the World. Among the companies that played there in the earlier years were the Wright Huntington and the Ernest Fisher Players, as well as groups carrying the Shubert name, some of them managed by Bainbridge, and some, too, enrolling members of his Minneapolis company. Later companies were identified with several directors, among them Arthur Holman and Cyril Raymond, and during one season, in 1931, the Women's City Club was a sponsor. At the older Metropolitan, L. N. Scott occasionally offset the increasing scarcity of road show companies by venturing into stock, in 1919 and again in 1921 engaging the Otis Oliver Stock Company.

Probably the most memorable stock enterprise in St. Paul during this period was the Arthur Casey Players, who in September of 1926 took over the President (the rejuvenated Orpheum Theater) and thrived reasonably well for three seasons and part of a fourth.

Mrs. Leslie Carter in *Zaza*

There was a brief blaze of glory in the spring of 1929, when a number of stars including Mary Boland, Mrs. Leslie Carter, and Guy Bates Post played guest engagements, but this did not prevent the company from folding shortly after the stock market crash, in November of that year.

From 1910 to 1930 the two Metropolitan Opera houses managed by L. N. Scott reaped from the "road" a crop whose yield, though diminishing, still spelled plenty in comparison with the famished decades that lay ahead. Only a few highlights can be mentioned such as Sothern and Marlowe in Shakespeare repertory and Robert Mantell's screaming Lear, and by contrast the violin-playing Hazel Dawn in *The Pink Lady*. Notable too were the visits of David Warfield in *The Music Master* and as Shylock, the quizzical Frank Bacon in *Lightnin'*, Otis Skinner in *Kismet*, and an Oriental spectacle from London, *Chu Chin Chow*. Maude Adams and Lionel and Ethel Barrymore had appeared on Minnesota stages in the 1900s, and soon came Laurette Taylor, Ruth Chatterton, and Jane Cowl, later to be followed by Katharine Cornell (in Michael Arlen's *The Green Hat*), Helen Hayes, Eva LeGallienne, and Alfred Lunt and Lynn Fontanne. The New York Theatre Guild was born and after an unsteady start was to exert a profound influence on the American theater's literary and artistic standards.

But even as the theater was gaining in maturity and power, with such writers as O'Neill, Elmer Rice, Sidney Howard, and Philip Barry supplying provocative plays for new productions, its old-time mobility stiffened, its "delivery service" to the country at large was reduced. High transportation costs and competition from Hollywood were shutting off from inland America the supply of Broadway plays. The institution of the "road" has never quite died out, and probably never will. But a generation was being born that would grow up without ever seeing, or only rarely seeing, a legitimate theatrical production.

Old theaters almost overnight became movie houses, restaurants, or parking lots. The Twin Cities lost their Metropolitans, although both had auditoriums that served in their places. The one in Minneapolis, converted into a theater, the Lyceum (on Eleventh Street), long had been the home of the Minneapolis Symphony. From the thirties on, these two houses sufficed to receive nearly all the dramatic productions exported at irregular intervals by New York and sometimes the Pacific coast.

After a few "turkeys" in the thirties and repeated visits of the Shuberts' unkillable *Blossom Time* and *Student Prince* companies, the road gave Minnesota the best, if not the most, of the professional theater. Costs and the increasingly selective audiences of the hinterland killed the second rate. Among the highlights of recent decades at the Lyceum (the later ones brought under the Theatre Guild subscription series) were Minnie Maddern Fiske in a farewell *Becky Sharp*, the Abbey Theatre Players from Dublin, a young unknown, Franchot Tone, in the bucolic *Green Grow the Lilacs* (later to blossom into the tuneful *Oklahoma!*), Maurice Evans in an uncut *Hamlet,* Eddie Dowling and Julie Haydon in

William Saroyan's *The Time of Your Life*, the Rodgers and Hammerstein musical hits, Frank Loesser's *Guys and Dolls*, Arthur Miller's *Death of a Salesman, Mister Roberts* by Minneapolis' Tom Heggen, Julie Harris in *The Member of the Wedding* and *The Lark*.

In 1958, legitimate plays in Minneapolis moved from their old and ill-favored home at the Lyceum to the more modern State Theatre on Hennepin Avenue, a movie house where for brief periods incoming plays displaced the film showings.

At this point our narrative is only half told, but the telling of the important other half must necessarily be short. The history of the amateur theater — the latter-day little theater movement, college and university dramatics, the "strawhat" summer seasons — is an immensely ramified one and much of it is obscure.

Amateur theatricals in Minnesota go back to Fort Snelling in the 1820s and to territorial St. Paul, where the German language theater found an early footing and flourished well into the eighties. Schlegel's translation of *Hamlet* was presented in 1882; the Milwaukee German Theater visited St. Paul in 1889. Scandinavian dramatic societies were formed, drawing on immigrant populations eager to speak and hear their own tongues in performances that preserved the ties, as did the singing societies, with homeland cultures. The Irish had their own plays in addition to the popular Irish romances and comedies produced for general consumption, and they developed a custom of staging them annually on St. Patrick's Day. "Parlor theatricals" were popular from the beginning, and church groups and debating societies occasionally tore a passion to tatters on improvised stages. As early as 1881, a University of Minnesota freshman class presented a melodrama for the edification of classmates and parents, and in 1895 what was to become the Minnesota Masquers was organized as the Dramatics Club. In 1924, no fewer than seven Minneapolis amateur companies took part in a short-play contest at the Shubert — three from the university campus, two from the MacPhail School of Music and Dramatic Art, and two civic groups of brief repute, the Portal Playhouse and the Studio Players.

In the field of college drama, a record of particular significance and quality has been achieved by the University of Minnesota Theater, whose direct forebears were campus dramatics clubs (chief of which was the Masquers), and the university's speech department headed by Frank M. Rarig. In 1915 a little theater had been constructed in Nicholson Hall basement, seven years later the first play was presented in what is now Scott Hall—Lord Dunsany's *If*—and the theater as now constituted was founded in 1931, when A. Dale Riley became director.

Riley continued in that post until his death in 1936. He was succeeded by C. Lowell Lees in 1937, the year that Frank M. Whiting joined the staff as technical director. When Lees left in 1943, the stage-wise, progressive Whiting took full charge and since then the theater has presented more than 200 plays. Annual Shakespeare performances, classics from ancient Greece and Rome, many original scripts, musical productions ranging from *Annie Get Your Gun* to Stravinsky, all have had their place on the distinguished and varied list offered through the years by the campus playhouse.

The University theater's audiences became international when acting companies were sent, under government auspices, to Europe and Brazil in 1957 and to the Orient in 1958. In 1958 too it acquired a floating theater, a river sternwheeler which it converted into a period-style showboat presenting, with huge success, Augustin Daly's melodrama *Under the Gaslight* in the Twin Cities and downriver Minnesota towns.

The honor of originating the little theater idea in America, and putting it into effect, goes to Duluth, which in November of 1914 organized a community playhouse. This, as far as the record shows, was the first of its kind. In the three preceding years Duluth's Drama League, a women's organization, had tried without much success to bring worthwhile plays to the city, which led finally to its sponsors' decision to perform their own plays. A Christian Science church served as a theater, pews were subscription seats, and a pulpit became the stage. Duluth's Little Theatre, later called the Duluth Playhouse, was the first in America to produce Shaw's

Frank M. Whiting   Don Stolz

The Dark Lady of the Sonnets, permission to stage it having been wheedled from G. B. S. himself. The theater's guiding spirit was Mrs. S. R. Holden, a friend of the Irish playwright Lady Gregory, who once visited Duluth at Mrs. Holden's invitation to see the theater and its work.

Inactive during America's participation in World War I, the theater resumed energetically after the Armistice, acquired its permanent home on Twelfth Avenue East in 1924 and engaged its first professional director, Maurice Gnesen. Its repertoire under Gnesen was rather overloaded with dour Russian offerings, but Duluth playgoers were privileged to see for the first time Gorky's *The Lower Depths* and Andreyev's *He Who Gets Slapped.* Several directors of outstanding ability, notably John Wray Young in the thirties, have guided its destinies since, and in 1956 a multiple director scheme was started whereby different local directors have been assigned different plays.

Theater 61, a quonset structure twelve miles beyond Duluth on the north shore, was operated from 1949 to 1956 by Paul Gilmore as a comedy theater, and in a subsequent and final season offered Broadway fare under a new management. Two other summer theaters in the resort areas, popular both with residents and vacationers, are the Nisswa Summer Theater near Brainerd and the Paul Bunyan Playhouse at Bemidji.

The state's outstanding and oldest "strawhat" is the Old Log Theater near Excelsior on Minnetonka's shores, directed by Don Stolz since 1941. In pleasant tree-shaded surroundings, this hardy institution, an Equity house, has steadily grown in quality and patronage, and each summer skims the Broadway "cream" of comedies and serious plays, often dipping into O'Neill, Molnar, Sherwood, and Tennessee Williams. Its casts have been a smooth blend of imported players and mature local talent.

The urban Twin Cities community has been served by numerous groups since the twenties, most of them of frail staying powers, a few more tenacious. The record for longevity is held by St. Paul's Edyth Bush theater, which also has the most attractive physical structure of any legitimate house in the state. The theater, in the Highland Village district, was built in 1940 by Mrs. Archibald Granville Bush, who in its earlier years played roles from time to time on its stage. The theater's schedule runs through the year, and its present director, Charles Meehan, has shown skill in selecting gifted amateurs and producing near-professional results in the plays they perform. In 1956 St. Paul acquired another community theater, Theater St. Paul, which started with performances in high school auditoriums and later purchased a former synagogue in which to present arena-type productions. Directed by Rex Henriot, the theater recently received a Hill Foundation grant with which to expand its operations.

In Minneapolis, the North Star Drama Guild had a brief but brilliant career in the late forties at the Woman's Club, with locally drafted casts supporting such luminaries as Lois Wilson, Sidney Blackmer, and Blanche Yurka.

Less pretentious in aim but longer lasting has been the first arena-style company in the city, the Theater in the Round Players, directed by Frederick Hilgendorf and mobilizing a zealous do-it-yourself aggregation of stagestruck laymen. Arena staging and the physical adaptation to a three-sided audience have resulted in some imaginative and striking productions.

A new and fruitful development has taken place in the metropolitan suburbs, with lively amateur groups springing up in Richfield, Bloomington, St. Louis Park, White Bear Lake, and Roseville.

Minnesota's "grass roots" movement in play production, its college and community activity, the growing hunger evident everywhere for "live" performances in an age of electronics and wide screens — all are hopeful portents. They are symptoms of an interest in theater not only undying but undergoing an exciting rebirth and revitalization.

᠎᠎᠎

I have borrowed considerably from my own book, *Music and Maestros: The Story of the Minneapolis Symphony Orchestra* (Minneapolis, 1952), in preparing the brief history of music in Minnesota. For the material on the very early period I owe much to Frances Densmore's discussion of *Songs of the Chippewa* (pamphlet accompanying Library of Congress Album XXII) and the recordings of Indian songs she made, a selection of which are available through the music division of the Library of Congress; to Grace Lee Nute's *The Voyageur* (New York, 1931); and to Theodore C. Blegen's *Norwegian Emigrant Songs and Ballads* (Minneapolis, 1936). I have also resorted gratefully to *A History of St. Olaf Choir* (Minneapolis, 1921) by Eugene E. Simpson and to *Music Master of the Middle West: The Story of F. Melius Christiansen and the St. Olaf Choir* (Minneapolis, 1944) by Leola Nelson Bergmann. Among the persons and institutions that have been of great assistance are the Minnesota Historical Society; the St. Paul and Minneapolis public libraries; Gladys Wilson, who is in charge of the music room at the Minneapolis library; Elsa Anneke, Duluth pianist; Orvis Ross, Rochester composer and conductor; and Harvey Waugh, music educator of St. Cloud; Russell Roth and Dick Maw of Minneapolis.

Much of the information in the informal history of the theater in Minnesota was gleaned from three doctoral theses in the University of Minnesota theater library—one by Frank M. Whiting on the St. Paul theater from its beginnings to 1890, another by Donald Z. Woods on the Minneapolis theater to 1883, and a third by Audley

M. Grossman on the Minneapolis theater from 1890 to 1910. Another valuable source of material was the article "Two Decades of Trouping in Minnesota, 1865–1885," by Andrew F. Jensen, in the June 1947 issue of *Minnesota History*. Of particular help in chronicling the heyday of stock in Minneapolis was Mrs. Marie Gale Bainbridge, who in addition to telling me much of interest made available her pressbooks covering the period. Among others who were of great assistance were Gilbert Fawcett of Duluth; James Taylor Dunn, librarian of the Minnesota Historical Society; Don Stolz of Minneapolis; Frank M. Whiting of Minneapolis; and Bradley L. Morison, who was drama critic for the *Minneapolis Tribune* during part of the Bainbridge regime at the Shubert Theater. The general reference works used include Glenn Hughes's *A History of the American Theatre, 1700–1950* (New York, 1951); Ward Morehouse's *Matinee Tomorrow: Fifty Years of Our Theater* (New York, 1949); Lloyd Morris's *Curtain Time: The Story of the American Theater* (New York, 1953); Cecil Smith's *Musical Comedy in America* (New York, 1950); and Phyllis Hartnoll's *The Oxford Companion to the Theatre* (London, New York, 1952).

John K. Sherman

has been covering the cultural front for the *Minneapolis Star and Tribune* for nearly 30 years. His range includes music, drama, dance, art, and books. In addition to reviewing local theatrical events, he goes to New York once each year to review the new shows there. He is the author of a book, *Music and Maestros: The Story of the Minneapolis Symphony Orchestra* (University of Minnesota Press), and is an amateur actor. One of his hobbies is bread baking. He has others, too, and he does occasional radio and television work. He has published free-lance material in the *Saturday Evening Post*. At the *Star and Tribune* his schedule for a typical week includes at least one book review, half a dozen recordings reviews, several play and concert reviews, a Sunday column on almost any subject, and the assembling of two arts pages.